CHRIS ARMSTRONG

Book of the

Spirit

curated lines publishing

Book cover design by Chris Armstrong

Book of the Spirit

Chris Armstrong

Rooted in the mythologies of religion, of church, synagogue and the Zen Buddhist temple or monastery, and calling, too, on the Graeco-Roman gods and muses, this collection borrows words, terminologies and phrases as well as their characteristic styles to resonate with the Christian and Jewish language and liturgies, with just a whisper of Far Eastern religions. Blending near identical theologies around a single belief system, a religion centred on love, there are echoes of the Old Testament of the Bible, and of the Torah, the Talmud, and Midrash and Kabbalistic teachings. For example, Kabbalistic teaching suggests that the manifestation of God that we perceive is his unity, when he transitions from nothing to one, just as Zen masters understand the nothingness of the godhead: a God present in nothingness. Despite this heritage, the collection speaks from - and for - the spirit of the modern world. It is the voice of our deepest, most primal faith.

The **Book of the Spirit** could be seen as a secular supplication or rogation to love and to the word—with a small 'w', the written word—to the ability to use words well with love, in praise. In praise of writing itself; in praise of the spiritual; in praise of love. As it is in the prophet Hosea, "Take with you words and turn to the Lord: say unto him..." (Hosea 14:2). Sing unto love. Sing unto the Gods.

Many of my traditional images, found in many of my poems and writings - time, the horizon, the sea - as well of course as love, find a place again in these lines - in my prayers.

Chris Armstrong
June 2022

Introit

Above the Horizon

these are the days in which we search for a new present and a new time
travels the ancient paths not quite at peace with our pilgrimage, the future

becomes nothing but a sunlit ripple in the dark eternal wash of the sea
forever closing with the present to vanish in the soft sands, wasted

as we drift to an unknown destination somewhere beyond our lives, the past,
a memory held only in each long lone look, captive in its rainbow window, fades,

becomes insubstantial and is forgotten as a new present envelops the isolated;
the moment's beaten path is the only focus of the day as we search the world for hope,

for a future, a new future, a better future, aware of time only in our memory until -
watching the sun sink below the horizon, time's illusory rim, and the vast sea

that is the circle of our future existence wash its unknown waves to our feet -
we understand the futility of the search, we understand each splash of destiny

Eternity Not Eternity

Each horizon that you see is your unattainable destiny
For only the ocean can know the horizon
And we are drops left on the shingle
Until the sea reclaims us for its own
Then you and I will be one in nothingness
Oh lover of my heart.
Ask nothing of the sun,
        its light will hide its wisdom
Ask nothing of the sea,
        for we are one with its depths:
Our selves absorbed within its endless border
Our lives drifted beyond its non-existent line
As a future - our illusion - flows towards us.
No stone can tell of our passing
        no sea strand sing of our morrows
For our souls are as atoms of that divine void, the sea
We are no longer; not you, oh my love, not I
        but neither are we become nothing -
Attār knew: the truth we seek is a sea without shores
        and paradise lies in a single drop.

Sunyata

Psalm

O sing unto Love!
When I have words, then shall I write
For my heart yearns to sing of my love -
O Thalia, I know only the sound of thought
        and I am become deaf.
Tempted, could I know what my hand would take -
        the burning coal or the gold?
Erato has stilled my lips, my tongue
        and holds my soul captive:
I can no longer form my lines.
O my love!
Should I call down my verses from the trees?
Or should I weep by the babbling stream,
        my unknown song held in its waters?
I have turned my Gods into nothingness
My soul embraces the void
I have turned my Gods into silence
My ear embraces the song
I have turned my Gods into stone
But the flint rock gives forth their words
        the air rings with their sacred song
And the rippled brook with the secret name of love -
I have turned my Gods into desire
My body is anointed with their passion.
Hineni

Spoken Psalm

Even as I was robed in words
I sang only silence
As the words fell from me
I was shackled to my nakedness:
My words turned sour on my lips
And I knew only a bitter song.
Come daughters of Mnemosyne
For I no longer know my words
Come heirs of Aoide
Descend from the dark
For now my voice is silent
Come, with Erato, to this holy place:
Only words can cover my naked skin.
Sisters of Mercy, compose my dull mind:
With Selene cast thy light on the darkness
Scribe thy words over all my flesh
Wake my tongue, and clothe me
In the language of thy light:
Without you I know no words:
For all that I conceive needs thy blessing:
Reveal words to me that please my ear:
Let me speak with a new voice
And sing a new song
Rejoicing in thy sacred vestment

Canticle

When I no longer have sorrow
Your spirit departs from my house.
Yet when I am mute and have no words,
When I am alone and lost, I cry out to you
From nothing, you become one with my pain.
Even as my meditations founder
And despair robs my pen of ink
I know that you will comfort me.
Wake me in the temple of your heart!
And let me sing in your holy sanctuary
For were we not one in righteousness
Fleeing before the face of the unjust?
Even in the darkest of times you were with me:
I dwelt in the stewardship of your house
And bathed my body in your waters
I have bowed down to your beauty
And knelt before your wisdom.
In my weakness lend might to my arm
And furnish my songs with joy;
Let your presence comfort me:
My body is naked without your counsel
Let words bloom on my flesh
And your grace clothe me.
When my silent voice weeps in the wilderness
You are the rock in my desert
Let my wasteland gladden and rejoice
For your spirit is eternal in me
And righteousness is immortal

Antiphon

Lift up your heart and sing with me!
For I, Aoide, am the word of love!
Poet! Let your voice remember me
And your song sound again over my temples;
Even as you know again the holiness of my sanctuary
Let my light open your eyes and my voice loose your tongue
Let your past be no more in your mind for now is a new land
Wherein I shall cause the arid plains to blossom
And deep river waters to cover your nakedness
That your body may soak in my name
People shall rejoice in your song
And their harps shall play in the new world
I shall awaken your tongue
And light shall shine on your body of words

Lift up your heart and sing with me!
Sing my words of love!

Hymn

Weep! For I have chained my Gods to silence
And my heart is deaf to their word
Weep! I have turned my Gods into nothing
For their words ever constrain me
Hineni ! Hineni!

I have no words to describe my love
For my words hold my Gods within my verse
I have turned my Gods into stone
But the flint rings with their sacred song
Hineni ! Hineni!

Sing! Let music flow in the desert
And brooks ripple with the secret name of love
I have turned my Gods into desire
And I know no words for them save love
Hineni ! Hineni!

Rejoice! For I have turned my Gods into love:
If I think of love then in my mind love *is*
And I can see no greater joy than love
Sing loud love lives: nothing can despoil love!
Hineni ! Hineni!

Prayer

Hear me, oh my Gods!
Though we have sung praises to our passion
My heart and my voice tremble before my Gods
Though I have turned my Gods into nothingness
So my soul may embrace the void
My pen is stilled by their might
Yet even as my Gods are like the flint rock in the desert
They give forth abundance
That my voice may sing praises
And celebrate the beauty of the word.
Yet the song is silenced in my heart
And my words are as nothing!
Have we not dwelt in the temples of love
And sung in the holy places?
Have I not bathed in your beauty
And bowed down in your waters
Hineni! We are here!
Let us now return to our Gods
For I know them in the void
Hineni! We are here!
Let my soul leave my pride on the other side
And my body leave there its desires
So that I may be blessed again with words
       Shantih shantih shantih

A Prayer for Deliverance

Hear me, oh my Gods!
In our prayers we call on the mercies of the Gods
That their light may shine from the vacuum
Over the blackness that spreads from the other side:
The evil darkness that would bring down our race!
I have turned my Gods into love
That their power may be like the dew unto Israel
To cover the land with fragrant bounty
So that we may revive as the grasses in Spring;
I have turned my Gods into silence
And my songs of love are quieted in the fields
I have turned my Gods into desire:
Even in your arms I know a need for more prayer
Even when I feel you hold me through the dark night
My body is weak and I have no words of love
Wake again my tongue and let the language of light
Be heard again throughout the world

Piyyut

Here, in the hills of the Land, beneath the mist clouds of the mountains,
In the valleys and beside the rivers let us sing many words of praise.
Never before have the waters given up the secret names of love:
Each word that covers my nakedness is like the ripple of a brook
Never before have the sanctified words of love felt so sweet -
In humility, I turn to my Gods from my silence knowing
  Love is beyond definition: I can never describe its holy name
  Or command the words offered to me in blessing by the waters, even these
  Reduce its power and its radiance touches yet does not touch our soul
  Diminishing our passion and quieting our songs of praise.

        All of the words which clothe me turn my Gods into nothingness
        My soul can only meditate on the vastness of their void
        Early in the day let us raise our voices and sing of the light:
        Night will descend silently on our prayers!

Song of Praise

Neither the babbling stream waters nor their flood
Can wash away my love nor o'erwhelm my desire
For I am my beloved's and she is in my heart
My right hand lies beneath her head
And my left hand embraces her
Whose lips are soft beneath my own
Neither my beloved nor my love will perish
For each day I have sought her out
                        in the agony of my doubts:
    Who will want and who will love
    Who by day and who by night
    Who by lust and who by passion
    Who by ease and who by trouble

Neither the heat of the day nor cool night's chills
Shall spoil our meeting nor temper our embrace
By night on our mattress have we sought each other
And by the light of day have we found love
For her body is sweet to touch and her hands
Are ever gentle in their embrace
Neither my beloved nor my love shall pass
For all my life have I known my love
                        in the agony of my doubts:
    Who in mountain wastelands and who at sea
    Who in the present time and who in distant days
    Who is naked and who is clothed
    Who by need and who by love

Neither the trials of life nor sacred death
Can destroy my love nor chill the blood in my heart
For as I hold my beloved close in my arms
Then she feels my passion and her lips find mine
As I once charted the seas, so I know her body
Whose deeps and shallows ripple beneath my love
Neither my beloved nor my love will weaken
For each moment with her is a day
                        in the agony of my doubts:
    Who will seek rest or who will quicken
    Who by calm waters and who by waves
    Who by mountain top and who by valley
    Who by precious love and who by eternity

Evensong

The poet said, "I have turned my Gods into desire"
And his words fell from him and he was naked
You who would judge him, love righteousness
    Priests! Sing praise unto Love!
    When words flow forth, then will the poet write
    For his heart will always sing of love
And the Gods said, "We have turned man into one of us"
And man knew love and was clothed in words
Let those who would judge his words, know wisdom
    Priests! Sing praise unto Love!
    When words dress love, then will the poet write
    For his heart will always sing of love
And the writer said, "I have turned my Gods into nothingness"
And in this true freedom, my words will fill the void
May priests who judge the creation, know the winds of space
    Priests! Sing praise unto Love!
    When words have space, then will the poet write
    For his heart will always sing of love
And the carpenter said, "I have turned my Gods into wood"
And held his destiny high for the people to see
For he needed them even as the righteous desire Gods
    Priests! Sing praise unto Love!
    When love flow forth, then will the poet write
    For his heart will always sing of love

Satori

The Carpenter

Amidst the sawdust and the shavings
in the low sun through a spider spun window
fine wood dust flies up, settling on every surface
glowing gold in the already golden light.

Then the rasp of the saw is replaced
by the rhythmic sound of a wood plane
and long shavings fall to the floor
curling around his feet -
pausing to test that his work is square
the man shifts his feet and the shavings rustle;
checking his marks he planes some more
the smell of the warm wood
strong in his nose
the feel of the pliant timber
silken to his thumb -
he is satisfied with his work.
Straightening and checking his marks again
he picks up a chisel
to tidy up the joint
and then smiles as he slots
the two pieces of wood together
inserts the locking dowels
and knocks them home.
Tomorrow will be the day:
he will sand it lightly
and add polish
buffing the surface
to a perfect finish -
then he will go forth
bearing his cross.

The carpenter knows
that he will always be remembered
for that perfect cross.

Eternity: a Ghazal

And in that moment the young man died a woman was left forlorn
The weight of her desolation borne on frail shoulders bent forlorn,

Become bowed crooked beneath her life's cruel dress, she is left careworn
Eternity became a black shawl and a black mossed dress forlorn

She sees her young God forsaken, laid low afore the naked thorn
Cold death lies in new turned mounded sod, from this moment left forlorn

The perfect lawn has become slick grey clay, shale of this grey damp morn
We only ask what garden holds death's dominion inhumed forlorn

And the sad woman so late reborn could only reply in scorn
All of the Gods lamented long within my arms this day forlorn

His loyal friends wept long where he lay beneath the iron black thorn
Knowing well every lost hour of the damping dark day forlorn

She knows the eternal mizzling mists of heaven will ever mourn
A son, settling soft to haze cruel spikes and blood-red haws forlorn

Their heartfelt ancient love of peace is now as lees left in the horn
All Zion's bitter tears can brook no relief for this man forlorn

As still they thought to hear his voice call out as of an echo borne
Soft in all the angels' prayers as riven-winged they fall forlorn

Power lay not in the strength of his arm but ever would adorn
His hushed and priestly verse, his old fables raised up by death forlorn

The First Winter

Three white swans stood beneath three thorn trees
In the cold of the day, having fasted to dawn:
They stood, their black feet stark on the white snow
While in my head my eyes white frozen in the gaze were
Ice blinded to all other detail of shore and field;
Yet mid-lake where the snow had melt-blended
I saw forged an uneven dimpled surface
Which caught a shine of brightness. And I heard God
Say, Shall these birds live? Shall these
Birds of snow live? And that which had sheltered them spoke rustling:
Because of the blood which I hold in my fruit
The goodness and strength of my thorns shall yet protect them
Even as the lake's white gown spreads
And the intense cold flows off the ice at my roots,
Its presence chilling as glacial wind.
Yet even while the stream from the high spring
Sparkles with winter's frazil so may they prosper
Beneath my crown for now am I grown up from the earth.
And the swans arched their necks
Who stood between the white and the white
And their eyes watched and knew
As I, awed, mute, thought
They stand in line like choristers
Before an empty crypt: poised but silent

Apocrypha

Paean

Once
soft light
gently glass stained
lit our dust in the air   (a dancing singing helix of new joy)
from dull clay, a carol   raised high
creating   celebrating
destiny.

Then,
their world argent
with each carminecry sigh   sigh in passion
epochs were new ceded   in love
heavens lain
light bright raised
on their altar.

Not. Not naught:
nascent
futures   destinies
a lone voice
a carol
in the cloister
dreaming. Once.

Vespers

As I pass beyond my summer wall
Once more the land embraces my spirit
And its silence becomes my prayer
While I and heaven hear
The wind whispered psalm
As dusk caresses the treetops
That surround my field fane -
I walk slowly through its grassy nave
Lost in my old memories
And pause at the far gate:
The sun sinks low behind me
And my long shadow stretches out in penance

Published by

————————————curated lines publishing———————————

Printed in Great Britain
by Amazon

12993240R00020